To all the sons and daughters-in-law who revel in the sound of laughter that accompanies family gatherings—this one's for you. "The Ultimate Joke Book about Mothers-in-Law" is a tribute to the unique relationship with in-laws. May this collection add a burst of laughter to your family events, lighten the moments of tension, and remind us all that a little humor goes a long way in maintaining family harmony. Here's to laughter, the best medicine of all!

The Ultimate Joke Book about Mothers-in-Law

By Frida Trumont

Why did my mother-in-law cross the road?

To prove she was right, as always!

I came across 6 men beating up my mother-in-law. My wife asked "aren't you going to help?" I said no. Six should be enough!

My mother-in-law said, "I'll dance on your grave." I replied, "I hope you do. I'm being buried at sea."

First man: "My mother-in-law is an angel."
Second man: "You're a lucky fella, mine's still alive."

What's the difference between outlaws and in laws?

Outlaws are Wanted.

Last week my wife and I went to buy a car and the salesman asked if I wanted an airbag. I said: "No thanks. I already have a mother-in-law."

My mother-in-law and I were happy for 20 years. Then we met.

I took my mother-in-law out today.

I love being a sniper!

My mother-in-law and I were happily chatting when she suddenly said, "You're like a son to me." Then she added, "No wonder I'm so disappointed."

First man "I took my dog to the vet today because it bit my mother-in-law."

Second man: "Did you put it to sleep?"

First man: "No, I had its teeth sharpened."

"My mother-in-law suffers from acute diabetes and hay fever... I always try to cheer her up with chocolate and flowers."

I can't wait to spend the rest of my life being judged by your mother.

What's my mother-in-law's favorite game?
Guessing why I'm wrong!

Man: "So, how long do you think you'll be staying with us?"
Mother-in-law: "Well... for as long as you like."
Man: "What, not even for coffee??"

My mother-in-law's calendar is pretty empty. It's just one big "Counting Days Until I Can Meddle Again" event.

I'm not saying the mother-in-law's ugly but she went to see that film the Elephant Man and the audience thought she was making a personal appearance.

"I bought my mother-in-law a chair for her birthday... but my wife wouldn't let me plug it in."

Anagram of "mother-in-law".

Woman Hitler

My mother-in-law has a new hobby – rearranging my life.

How many mothers-in-law does it take to change a light bulb? One. She just holds it up there and waits for the world to revolve around her.

First man: "Where's your mother-in-law?"

Second man: "She's in the garden."

First man: "Where? I can't see her."

Second man: "You have to dig a little."

My mother-in-law asked, 'If you don't like me, why do you take me on holiday with you?'. I told her, 'so I don't have to kiss you goodbye…'

Why is my mother-in-law like a GPS? She always knows which way I should go!

My mother-in-law fell down a wishing well. I was amazed. I never knew they worked.

My mother-in-law is a multitasker. She can make you feel unwelcome and judged all at once.

A man threw his mother-in-law into the lion's den at the zoo. He's being sued by the SPCA for cruelty to animals.

"I don't know what I'd do without my mother-in-law, but it's nice to dream about it."

I never forget a face, but in my mother-in-law's case I'm willing to make an exception.

My mother-in-law's cooking is so bad, the flies pitched in to fix the window screen.

My mother-in-law has weekly sessions with Lucifer on how to be even more vicious. I've no idea what kind of fees she's charging him.

My mother-in-law is an excellent gardener. She specializes in planting seeds of doubt in my mind.

Lawyer: "Your mother-in-law passed away in her sleep. Shall we order burial, embalming or cremation?"

Son-in-law: "Take no chances. Order all three."

Wife: "This wine is described as full bodied and imposing with a nutty base, a sharp bite, and a bitter aftertaste."

Husband: "Are you describing the wine or your mother?"

Adam and Eve were the happiest, and luckiest, couple in the world, because neither of them had a mother-in-law.

What's my mother-in-law's favorite exercise? Jumping to conclusions.

Police Officer: "Sir, it looks like your mother-in-law has been hit by a bus."

Man: " I know, but she has a great personality."

My mother-in-law is a minimalist.

She minimizes any chance of us getting along!

I always know when it's the mother-in-law knocking at the door because the mice start throwing themselves on the traps.

"My mother-in-law says I should bury myself in my work. I drive a cement mixer."

My mother-in-law's coming. I had to clear out half my closet so she has somewhere to hang upside down and sleep…

Got my mother-in-law a cemetery plot for Christmas and the next year didn't buy her anything. When she asked me why I didn't buy a gift for her I said........ because you still haven't used the one I got you last year.

I asked my mother-in-law if she's familiar with the phrase 'personal space.' She said, "Yes, it's that area I invade whenever I visit."

How many mothers-in-law does it take to ruin a marriage? Just one…mine!

"I live in constant fear that my Latina mother-in-law will be deported. Who lives at 324 3rd St. Los Angeles. She gets off at 6."

Every time I'm with my mother-in-law, I wonder who's running Hell in her absence.

I've spent more than four years looking for my mother-in-law's killer. But I can't find anyone to do it!

My mother-in-law's gift-giving philosophy: One size fits nobody.

I took my mother-in-law to Madame Tussaud's Chamber of Horrors, and one of the attendants said, 'Keep her moving sir, we're stock-taking'

My mother-in-law has gone a bit off the rails.
Hopefully the train still gets her.

"My mother-in-law asked for her birthday 'something for in bath'. Too bad she didn't like my toaster..."

I still remember my mother-in-law's last words before she died.

She said, "Stop shaking the ladder you idiot!"

Wife: "There is a burglar downstairs in the kitchen and he is eating the cake that my mother made for us."

Husband: "Who shall I call, the police or an ambulance?"

Employee: "Can I have a day off next week to visit my mother-in-law?"
Boss: "Certainly not."
Employee: "Thank you so much! I knew you would be understanding."

Son: "Dad, what was the name of Adam's mother-in-law?"

Father: "He didn't have a mother-in-law, son, he lived in paradise."

My mother-in-law's favorite saying: "You can't choose your family, but you can choose to criticize them."

I'm not saying the mother-in-law's ugly, but she uses her bottom lip as a shower cap.

First man: "If a tiger was attacking your wife and mother-in-law at the same time and you could save one, who would it be?"

Second Man: "The tiger of course. There are only a few left."

A 17 in blackjack is like a mother-in-law. Sometimes you want to hit it, but it's probably smarter not to.

Wife: "Can my mother come down for the weekend?"

Husband: "Why?"

Wife: "Well, she's been up on the roof two weeks already."

"The police have just released my mother-in-law after questioning her about the murder of her husband. They only spoke to her for two minutes before concluding he committed suicide."

What do a slinky and your mother-in-law have in common? They're both fun to watch tumble downstairs.

Why Did the mother-in-law cross the road?

She thought it was a boundary.

"If your mother-in-law and a lawyer were drowning and you had to choose…"

"Would you go to lunch or a movie?"

Did you hear about the roman fighter who ate his mother-in-law?

Terrible indigestion but he was gladiator.

My mother-in-law thinks she's psychic. She predicts all my failures.

"I'm trying to get my mother-in-law to go ice fishing before the ice gets too thick."

What do you do when you miss your mother-in-law?

Reload, aim, shoot again!

What does your mother-in-law and turkey have in common?
Seeing them once a year at Christmas is the perfect amount.

Boss: "Oh, I didn't expect you at work today, isn't it your mother-in-law's funeral today?"
Man: "Well you know how it is. Work first, then fun."

"My mother-in-law told me that beauty is only skin deep. She must have been born inside out..."

"It was very difficult to switch off my mother in law's life support system. I had to fight my wife and two doctors to do it."

"I really do have a soft spot for my mother-in-law. It's out in the garden behind the garage."

"My mother-in-law began to address the elephant in the room. I asked her why she was talking to herself."

Pharmacist: "In order to buy arsenic you need a prescription. A picture of your mother-in-law just isn't enough.'"

What do you call it when you're late to dinner at your mother-in-law's?

Delaying the inedible.

Why do they bury mother-in-law's 18 feet down instead of the normal 6 feet?

Because deep down, they really are nice people.

"I have a daughter named after my mother-in-law. Passive-Aggressive Psycho turns 5 next week."

"I had dinner with my mother-in-law the other night. Was gonna ask 'Would you to pass the salt, please?' But instead my tongue twisted and I said 'You stupid cow. You've completely ruined my life.'"

Afterword

Whether you picked up this book out of curiosity, desperation, or simply a love for laughter, I hope it brought a smile to your face and perhaps even a chuckle or two.

As you close this book, I encourage you to take a moment to appreciate the mother-in-law in your life, for all her wisdom, humor, and yes, even her quirks. And the next time you find yourself in a situation worthy of a joke, remember to laugh, because laughter truly is the best medicine, especially when it comes to family.

If you've enjoyed this collection, be sure to explore other titles in "The Ultimate Joke Book Series." Each book takes a lighthearted look at different professions, sports, and everyday situations, offering endless opportunities to chuckle and share the mirth with others.

Happy joking!

Frida Trumont

Printed in Great Britain
by Amazon